Wilderhope to Wall

The Parish of Rushbury at the turn of the Millennium

Acknowledgements of Financial Contributions

The Rushbury and District Records Trust gratefully acknowledges the generous contributions of the following people and organisations:

Brook House Farm
The W A Cadbury Trust
Coates Farm, Bed and Breakfast
East Wall Garage
Gilberries Cottage, Bed and Breakfast
Gilberries Hall Farm, Bed and Breakfast
Horseshoe Crafts
Colin Jones
John Lea, Agricultural Contractor
Merle Lippit, Rushbury School
Longmynd Service Station
The Millichope Foundation
Mullock & Madeley, Surveyors, Agricultural Valuers & Auctioneers
The Plough Inn

Brenda Pogson
Shell Better Britain Campaign
Shropshire Building Supplies
Shropshire Country Brides
Shropshire Hills Countryside Unit
Shropshire Rural Development Programme (Delegated Project Fund)
Stanway Fabrics
Stretton School of Dance
Michael Webster
Wenlock Spring Water Company
W C Wright & Son, Estate Agents
The Youth Hostels Association, Wilderhope Manor

Wilderhope to Wall

The text and most of the pictures were provided by the people of the Parish of Rushbury, through their many reminiscences and from the archives of the Rushbury and District Records Trust. Specific contributors to this book are: Neil and Veronica Cossons, Geraldine, Jacob and Roger Davies, Diana Dixon, Laurie Donnison, John Henderson, Chris Hotchkiss, Doreen James, Alf Jones, Meg Jones, Steve Jones, Joy Kohn, Jim Madeley, Brenda Pogson, Barbara Pugh, Val Sagar, David and Diana Taylor, John and Renée Webster, and Rowena Woodhead. The authors have made every effort to ensure that the information in this book is accurate, however, we apologise if there are any omissions or inaccuracies.

First published 1999

All rights reserved. No part of this publication may be reproduced, stored in a retrieval system, or transmitted, in any form or by any means, electronic or mechanical, by photocopying, recording or otherwise, without prior permission in writing from the publisher.

A catalogue record for this book is available from the British Library.

ISBN 0 9536758 0 7

Typeset in Times New Roman by Steve Jones
and printed in England by Craven Design & Print, Craven Arms
for the Rushbury and District Records Trust

Cover pictures: Front.   View across Ape Dale from Stone Acton – 1999.
Back.   View across Ape Dale from Wenlock Edge - 1988.

Published by:

The Rushbury and District Records Trust, c/o Rushbury CE School, Rushbury, Shropshire SY6 7EB, England

Wilderhope to Wall

CONTENTS

	Page
Introduction	4
Location and Geology	6
Flora and Fauna	10
Plan of Rushbury Village	15
Rushbury Church and Rectory	16
Rushbury School	21
Wall under Heywood	25
Longville in the Dale	31
East Wall	34
Stanway	37
Lushcott	38
Wilderhope	40
Buildings and Roads	42
The Train Comes and Goes	45
Rushbury Village Hall	49
Rushbury and Cardington Women's Institute	50
Longville Branch National Farmers' Union	51
Rushbury and Cardington Young Farmers Club	52
Rushbury and Cardington YFC – Memories	54
Food Glorious Food	56
Sheep Watch by Joy Kohn	62
Map of the Parish	63
Conversions of Units of Measurement	64

Wilderhope to Wall

INTRODUCTION

The Parish of Rushbury lies at the foot of Wenlock Edge in the valley of Ape Dale between Church Stretton and Much Wenlock. It has an area of about nine square miles or some 6,000 acres (2,400 hectares) and includes the village of Rushbury and the hamlets of Wall under Heywood, East Wall, Longville, Stanway, Lushcott and Wilderhope as well as several outlying smaller communities. In 1801, the date of the first national census, the population of the parish was 356. By the time of the 1881 census it had risen to 500, but a century later it had fallen again, to 436. In 1998 the population of the parish stood at 547.

The literal meaning of Rushbury is the 'rushy fort' which may refer to the existence of a fortified place in or near the village in Norman times. The first actual reference to Rushbury is in the Domesday survey of 1086 when the manor was in the hands of Roger de Lacey who sub-let to a fellow Norman by the name of Odo. It was a fairly prosperous settlement with five hides of land, a mill, a wood capable of fattening 40 swine and a falcon's eyrie.

From earliest times the main occupation of the people of the parish has been based on agriculture. That is the case today although an increasing proportion of the population now living in the parish work further afield, engaged in a wide variety of activities. This trend seems likely to continue. In the parish itself there are several light industries and non-agricultural enterprises including a

View north east along Wenlock Edge. The collection of White buildings in the foreground is Eaton. The line of white buildings middle left are between Rushbury and Wall under Heywood.
Photo: Clwyd/Powys Archaeological Trust

transport firm, coach company, two public houses, some bed and breakfasts, a bridal-wear centre, several poultry farms, a garage, agricultural contractor and a plant nursery.

The parish of today has been shaped by its long history. On ancient rocks, some over 600 million years old, is a landscape shaped only some 10,000 years ago at the end of the last ice age. There is evidence of Ape Dale's earliest inhabitants in the defensive ditches and banks of Caradoc, indications of the Roman occupation, and in Rushbury itself the circular earth mound of a small castle built perhaps a thousand years later. The earthworks of the nineteenth century can be seen in the line of the old railway, which closed within living memory, while in the church are the memorials to those men of the parish whose lives were cut short by the two world wars of the twentieth.

Today this quiet Shropshire parish is seen by visitors, as well as those who live here, as a place of peace, of great beauty and of tranquillity. But above all it is a living community where people go about their lives as they have always done, aware of their past, but with eyes firmly focussed on the future.

This book was prompted by the new millennium and the wish to put on record a view of the Parish of Rushbury just before the year 2000. It is the work of the people of the parish, who have written the text and whose reminiscences present a personal picture of the area in the last half-century or so of the second millennium.

Wilderhope to Wall

LOCATION AND GEOLOGY

The Parish of Rushbury is in south central Shropshire in the administrative area of the South Shropshire District Council, which has its head offices in Ludlow. The area forms part of the rural West Midlands of England, but physically it is more correctly part of the south Shropshire hills which form the eastern foothills of the Welsh massif.

The parish lies almost entirely in Ape Dale (the valley of the bees) which runs from north-east to south-west between Wenlock Edge and the Stretton Hills. For the most part, the Rushbury parish boundary follows stream courses and field hedges (some of which have been uprooted), dividing it from the adjoining parishes of Cardington to the north, then through east, south and west, the parishes of Easthope, Shipton, Munslow, Eaton-under-Heywood and Hope Bowdler.

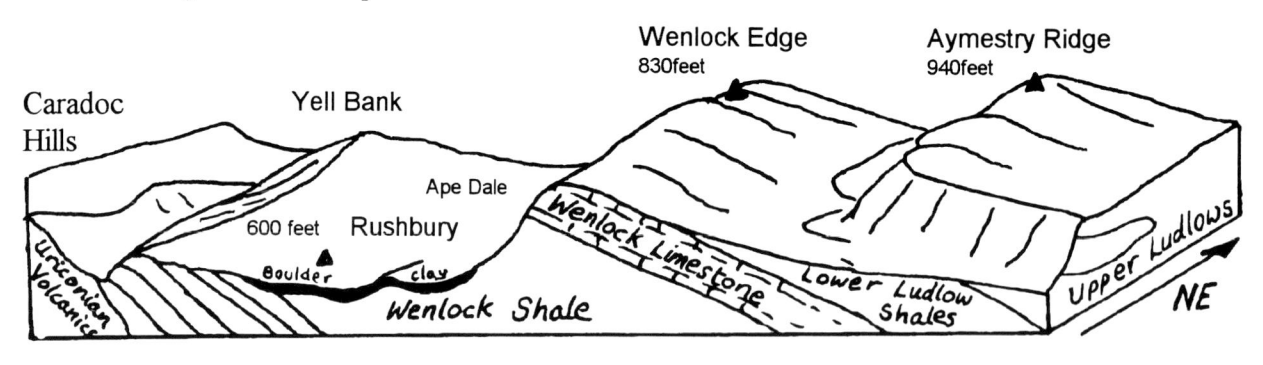

The underlying rocks or solid geology lie in chronological order from north-east to south-west, the oldest being to the north (see diagram of three dimensional view). The Pre-Cambrian rocks of Cardington Hill are the oldest, found in the area above Stone Acton. These were formed as the result of volcanic activity more than 600 million years ago and are referred to as Uriconian rock, after the local Roman settlement of that name. Owing to the intensity of earth movements since those times the strata is now folded and faulted into a complicated series that only the specialist can begin to understand.

Next in the series, at less than 600 million years old, are the Cambrian rocks, named after an ancient Welsh tribe. Exposures can be seen to the right of the road from Stone Acton towards Cardington at Hill End.

Wilderhope to Wall

During early Cambrian times an ocean extended as far as what are now the lower slopes of the Caradoc Hills, and Wrekin quartzites were formed (to be found at Hill End), followed by Comley sandstone and shale deposits. One of the earliest trilobite fossils was found in Comley quarry near Botvyle. At the youngest end are the Shineton shales, visible in the stream bed about half a mile to the south of Cardington mill. An attempt was made earlier this century to quarry part of Hill End for road stone but the material was not very satisfactory.

Ordovician strata are the next in sequence and were formed about 500 million years ago. This underlying rock extends across the area from near the Court House then past the Gilberries through to Wall Bank and beyond. The best exposure is at Soudley quarry. The texture and fine quality of the stone suggest that the sediments were deposited in quiet and moderately deep water. Many buildings in the district are constructed with this material, easily recognisable by dark purple or chocolate-coloured banding in the brown stone.

Finally, by far the largest area of underlying strata around Rushbury is the Silurian, some 440 million years old. Here again the rocks were named after ancient Welsh tribes, the Ordovices and Silures. Wenlock Edge and parallel ridges form a major part. These rocks are derived from sediments deposited in a shallow sea during warm continental conditions. Wenlock Edge can be likened to a reef formed from the fossil remains of crustaceans and corals. Rich in calcium, the escarpment has been extensively quarried near Much Wenlock for lime, both for agricultural and building purposes and hardcore. So, the bones of the past, through the spreading of lime to raise the pH value of the soil, are used to strengthen the bones of the future through milk!

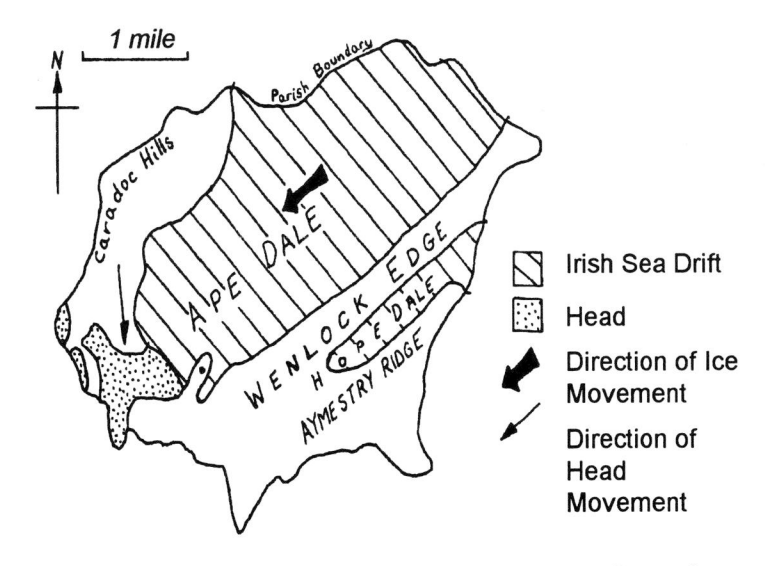

Over the millions of years since these rocks were formed there has been continental drift and the climate has

Wilderhope to Wall

fluctuated many times between tropical and glacial conditions. Those changes continue; it is only some ten thousand years since the glaciers of the last ice age retreated, as a result of variations in climate. During the last ice age, the arctic ice extended south to cover much of Europe and most of the British Isles. The polar regions of today are relics of that ice age. In places, the ice was many hundreds of metres thick and, like any glacier, the movement sculpted and scarred the landscape moving rocks and debris great distances. As a result, much of the landscape we see in and around Rushbury today was formed, quite recently, by ice and the melt-water associated with its retreat.

As the climate changed and the ice melted, the suspended material was dumped in-situ leaving mounds or hills on the valley floors. Brockhurst at Church Stretton is one example and Rushbury is another. The outwash at the snout or foot of the glacier left deposits of sand or gravel or both. In some areas these deposits are commercially worked as in the area between Dorrington and Bayston Hill. In Rushbury, patches of sandy soil can he found on land at the back of the houses in Rushbury Road, Wall, and these extend intermittently towards Ticklerton via the Saplings.

The melt-water eventually formed a huge lake across the lowlands of Shropshire and the Cheshire gap. It reached a depth of 100m and penetrated the Vale of Hughley almost to Longville but did not spill over the Longville watershed into Ape Dale. As the levels built up against Wenlock Edge the water finally broke through, cutting the deep chasm now called the Ironbridge Gorge. Elsewhere the massive outflows of water deepened the valleys creating the 'batches' around the Stretton Hills. All over south Shropshire there are valleys which appear too large for the streams that flow through them because they were cut by the huge volumes of water at the end of the last ice age.

Wenlock Edge at this time was the most important watershed in the country. The River Severn, having previously headed north to the Cheshire Plain and Mersey Estuary, switched south through the Ironbridge Gorge to link with the Stour at Stourport and flow south to the Bristol Channel. The drainage pattern of the minor streams was also affected in varying degrees. After the ice, Ape Dale was covered with boulder clay, alluvium and silt around streams and flood plains. The relief of the land varies from around the 300m contour at Cardington Hill and Hill End, falling to about 150m south-west of Rushbury on the valley floor. It then rises again to over 270m at the highest point of the Wenlock Edge to the north-east of Roman Bank. The rainfall pattern reflects the relief but at Rushbury, at about 250m above sea level, it averages something over 100cm per year. In an area that is frequently damp, local radiation fogs occur, particularly late in the year.

Wilderhope to Wall

Some parts suffer from inversion frosts, especially along the upper slopes of the Wenlock Edge escarpment and other northerly-facing pockets on hills. The average duration of the growing season, (i.e. when the mean monthly temperature is above six degrees, is about 240 days in the lower parts of the parish, or from the last week in March to the second week in November. In the higher areas, at about 250m, it is about twelve days shorter. The warmer rain-bearing prevailing winds sweep up Ape Dale from the Craven Arms direction, whereas in winter cold chilling winds blow from the north-east from the direction of Longville.

Human activity in Neolithic times (about 1700 BC) was restricted to hill tops - as evidenced by earthwork camps on the Caradoc and Longmynd - largely because the clay soils of the valleys encouraged dense forest unsuitable for settlement. It is reasonable to assume that the early settlers would roam the hills as far as Hill End and may have penetrated a little way into the forests of Ape Dale in their quest for food.

By the time of the Roman invasion the local tribes were using iron tools and weapons and had begun to occupy the lowlands as primitive methods of farming were devised. Some of these ancient peoples retreated westwards in the face of the Romans, to avoid subjugation, but others intermingled with the invaders. Shropshire boasted the fourth largest city in Roman Britain, Viroconium or Wroxeter, home to 6,000 men and the largest settlement to have escaped subsequent development. Remains of the roads built by the Romans can be found in and around the Parish of Rushbury. From Acton Burnell, following the line of the Lawley, Caradoc and Ragleth hills is a Watling Street spur of a Roman paved road, some 4m wide - Bot Street. Another branch from Acton Burnell, passing via Causeway Wood, enters the parish near Gretton and continues to Stone Acton before crossing Ape Dale through Rushbury and over Roman Bank. The area of Rushbury itself may have had a Roman settlement in Bury field to the north of the church. Could this have been the Roman Station, Bravinium?

The Saxons who followed the Romans must have looked for suitable sites to live. Incomplete woodland clearance favoured nucleated settlements for communal protection of livestock against wild animals and raiders. Rushbury and Wall were ideal, standing on elevated ground but with water readily available. The Saxons were established some 500 years before the Norman Conquest because, by the Domesday Record of 1086, the chief villages of today, including Rushbury, were already in existence.

Wilderhope to Wall

FLORA AND FAUNA

The entire parish of Rushbury lies in a designated Area of Outstanding Natural Beauty. It is dominated by the steep scarp slope of Wenlock Edge with its defining line of woodland stretching continuously from north-east to south-west as far as the eye can see. The Edge is one of the great landscape features of Shropshire and is of particular wildlife interest. It is composed in the main of limestone and calcareous shales and clays and these have been important in determining the nature of the vegetational cover. On the steeper slopes of the scarp there has almost certainly been woodland continuously since Britain emerged from the last ice age. Although much has been replanted with conifers there are still considerable stands of ancient deciduous woodlands and their colours, changing with the seasons, form a backdrop not only to the parish of Rushbury but to the whole of Ape Dale. Virtually all the parish can be seen from clearings in the trees along the crest of Wenlock Edge providing views across the dale to the Stretton Hills and Caradoc. Here the horizons are treeless but seasonal change is equally spectacular as the bracken turns from dark green to bright chestnut brown.

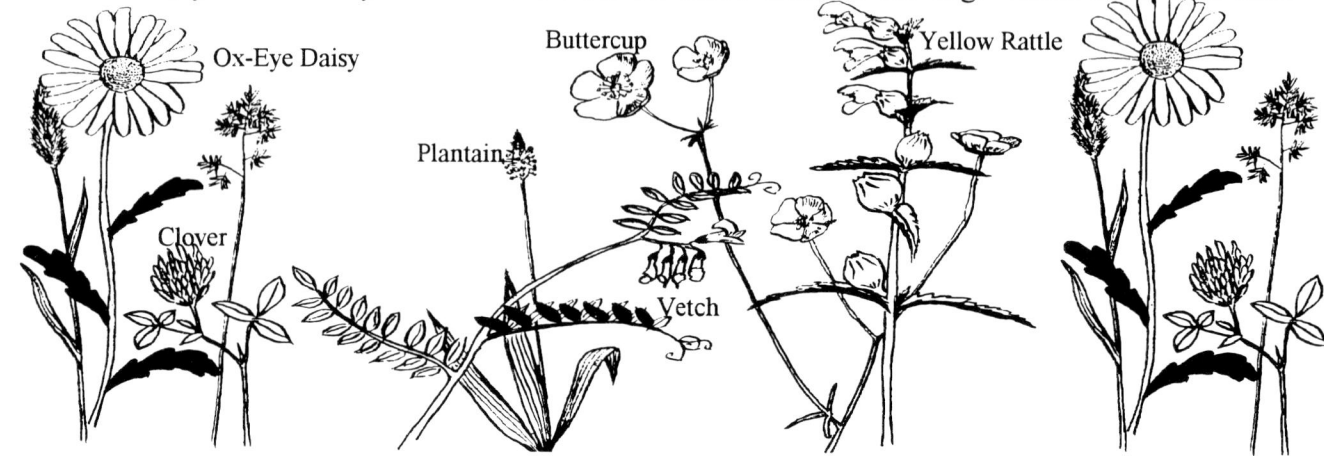

The flora of Wenlock Edge is exceptionally rich, especially in lime-loving plants. Of the native trees the ash rather than the oak is dominant, although both are widespread. Ash can be found throughout the parish and regenerates readily, rapidly taking over areas like the alignment of the old railway where there is no regular management. Elsewhere there are scattered small-leafed limes, wild cherry, wild service trees, yew and holly. Beneath the trees on those areas of the edge which have been little disturbed are typical limestone shrubs such as spurge laurel, spindle, guelder rose, field maple and dogwood. Other notable species include herb Paris, yellow bird's nest, autumn gentian, wood vetch, rock stonecrop, wood barley, and at least twelve different species of orchids. In the darker areas of the woods few ground plants thrive but those that do include dog's mercury and cuckoo pint. The animal and bird life is similarly limited to a few resident goldcrests, chaffinches and the occasional fox and badger.

The more open woodland is characterised by areas that may have once been pasture. These have regenerated naturally with ash and oak interspersed with occasional hawthorn and blackthorn bushes that may be remnants of old hedges. Other indicators of a pastoral origin to the woodland are aromatic meadowsweet, devil's-bit scabious, with its distinctive purple flower head, and the familiar three-lobed leaves of the red clover.

On the edge of the parish, at Marked Ash on the top of the dip slope of Wenlock Edge, are three traditionally managed herb-rich meadows. They are of particular interest for a type of grassland characterised by crested dog's-tail and common knapweed - but rich in a wide range of other species - which is now very scarce in Shropshire and in decline nationally. The meadows support a number of species which are either uncommon or rare in Shropshire, such as adder's tongue, common spotted-orchid, dyer's greenweed, common twayblade and meadow saffron. The meadows are separated by a

Wilderhope to Wall

stone track with wide grassy verges. These verges support a grassland flora almost as diverse as the meadows, including the locally uncommon gromwell. In fact, such has been the loss of unimproved grassland in south Shropshire, and especially on Wenlock Edge, that the Marked Ash meadows were designated as a Site of Special Scientific Interest by English Nature on 18 August 1998.

Another part of the parish that is particularly rich in wild flowers is Rushbury churchyard. Traditionally, God's acre of ground was enclosed around the church for the graveyard, this at a time before any modern land improvements had taken place. We have been left with a legacy of the flowers that would have been common a thousand years ago.

Oaks are widespread throughout the parish but are especially abundant along parts of the Edge. Some are ancient but few if any date from before man's active intervention in clearance for pasture or timber. Galls can frequently be found on the leaves, as evidence of the more than fifty gall-producing insects that live on oak trees. Oak apples, marble and spangle galls are the most common. In June the oak roller caterpillar often strips the leaves from the trees, unless the rooks remove the caterpillars first. This loss is made up by the 'lammas' growth, a summer flush of reddish young leaves so coloured to protect them from the sun.

In the more open woodland the ground cover supports a wider range of birds and animals including three species of woodpecker, treecreeper, willow tit, coal tit, long-tailed tit, black cap, chiffchaff and deer, badger, fox, hedgehog, stoat and weasel. Bramble, honeysuckle, sanicle, enchanter's nightshade and wood anenome are common and there are some prolific coverings of bluebell. The woolly thistle penetrates Shropshire from the south only as far as the limestones of Wenlock Edge. One of the rarer and more unusual trees is the native black poplar, which is found in a number of isolated pockets in Shropshire and is well represented in the parish. Individual trees can be found in a number of places and there is an important group at Stanway.

Most of the rest of the parish lies in Ape Dale which historically was damp and marshy, drained by the Eaton Brook and its tributaries on their way south-west to join the River Onny. Most of this area is in farmland although there are woods and abundant hedgerows providing a rich variety of plant species. A sinister newcomer to these wetter areas is the mink, a serious danger to the native water vole.

Wilderhope to Wall

Notable introduced species are the spectacular Scots pines in and around the churchyard at Rushbury which signal the centre of the village from a distance. The tallest of these, with its characteristic top-knot, is significantly higher than the tower of the parish church. Most of these trees were probably planted in the middle years of the last century by the Reverend Hotham as part of his improvements to the church and extensions to the rectory. Several are now past maturity and the loss of two in the churchyard as a result of autumn gales in 1996, one blown down and the other felled in the interests of safety, may mean that others will go in the near future.

Birds

Of the bird population of the Rushbury area the buzzard is the most spectacular. As the rabbit population revives in the aftermath of myxomatosis and as organochlorine residues continue to diminish so the buzzards return in increasing numbers. Rushbury is at the north-eastern edge of the great stronghold of buzzards in south Shropshire but they can be frequently seen throughout the parish and in the spring their loud mewing defines their territories, especially at the boundaries of the Wenlock Edge woodland and the open country to the west where they hunt for rabbit.

Spotted Flycatcher

More than 65 different species of birds are found in the Rushbury area. In the garden, one of the most common family of birds is the tit family. The robin, dunnock and wren, all insect eaters, are very common there as well. The finch family feeds on seeds, fruit and buds around the garden and includes the chaffinch, the greenfinch, the bullfinch, the goldfinch and, more recently, the siskins. Summer visitors include the warbler family, and the graceful swallows, swifts and martins. Another interesting summer visitor to watch is the spotted flycatcher, how it sits on a post or branch, darts out to catch an insect, and flies back to eat it, an action exclusive to flycatchers. Sometimes if there is a garden pond with fish in, a heron might come and eat them, and if the pond is large enough, there may be be mallards and moorhens. A lucky garden would have a tawny owl nesting in it, but owls stay mostly in the woodland.

Dipper

Wilderhope to Wall

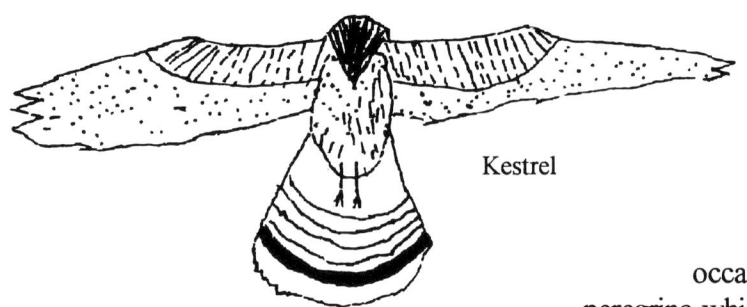

The most common bird of prey in the area is probably the kestrel, which is seen most often perched on telegraph poles or hovering, scanning the ground for mice or insects. Other day raptors are the sparrowhawk and occasionally the relatively small merlin, and the peregrine which comes down to pounce at great speeds. The night raptors are the hooting tawny owl, famous for its 'tu-whit, tu-whoo' quavering call, the near white barn owl, and the little owl which has superb night-vision like the other owls. The main packhorse bridge over Eaton Brook is very good for sighting water birds: Dippers, beautiful kingfishers and herons have been sighted in the brook from there.

Kestrel

There are various birds on the farmland. Lapwings and curlew visit often and very occasionally some snipe although they are quite hard to see because of their excellent camouflage. The song that sounds like, 'a little bit of bread and no cheese' is well known to be of the yellowhammer, a seed-eater of hedgerows and farmland. Members of the crow family seen in the farmland are the carrion crow, the rook, the magpie and the jay. Often buzzards can be seen feeding for insects on fields, for example Barn Ground. Wood pigeons and collared doves are very common and infamous for destroying large amounts of crops.

Curlew

When drumming is heard in Rushbury woodland and copses you know there must be either a greater or lesser spotted woodpecker about. They drum either as a call, to drill a hole for a nest site, or to get insects to eat. The green woodpecker has not got such a strong beak, so it probes into decaying trees, or the ground. An interesting bird to watch in copses and woods is a treecreeper as it flies down to the base of a tree, then creeps up the trunk searching for insects, and then flies down to the base of the next tree and does it again. You might see a sparrowhawk as it flies low through the wood after small animals and birds. Rarer species that may be seen in the area include: lesser spotted woodpecker, little owl, barn owl, snipe, peregrine, Canada goose, cuckoo, kingfisher, merlin, redstart and hobby.

Wilderhope to Wall

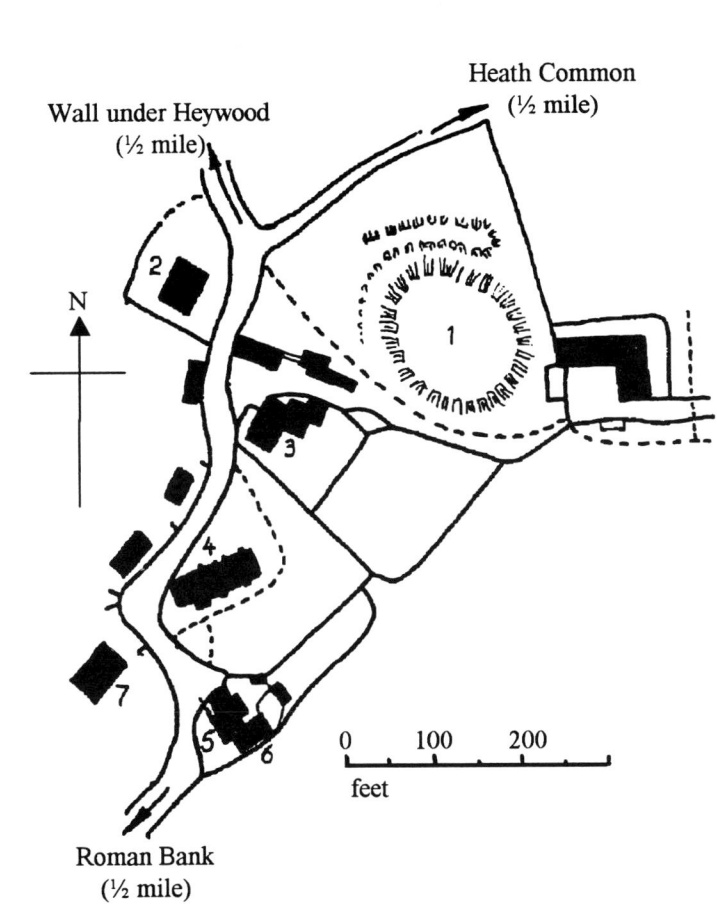

Plan of Rushbury Village Circa 1900

1. Saxon or Roman Earthworks
2. Tudor Manor House
3. Church Farm (1597)
4. St Peter's Church
5. School House
6. School
7. Rectory

Wilderhope to Wall

RUSHBURY CHURCH AND RECTORY

The Building of Rushbury Church

The main elements of the church that we know today - the tower, the nave and the chancel - have been little altered in the last 800 years. The historian Eyton says that the de Laci barons founded it after the Norman Conquest and gave it to Hereford Priory, but some masonry is Anglo-Saxon, which may suggest that it is earlier. The nave appears to have been built first, and around 1200 the chancel and the lower part of the tower were added. In 1793 the church was described as follows:

'The Church is of stone, in part plastered and in part whitewashed on the outside. There are some modern windows in the Church: all unsuitable in form and some whimsical. There are three narrow Gothic windows in the East end, which have a beautiful appearance on the inside. There is some old painted glass in them. The Church and chancel have an air of spaciousness. The former has 29 pews very irregular; the latter 2. Under the Belfry is a platform a little raised, with a table in the middle and benches round. This is used as a sort of gallery'.

St Peter's Church

The main restoration - very much at the same time as dramatic adaptations were made to the rectory - took place in 1855. A south vestry was built; the south porch was replaced; the top of the tower was rebuilt; seven buttresses were added; and all windows later than 1200 were replaced in the thirteenth century style. Internally, new benches and woodwork were provided and the church was retiled. More recently, a tower screen was added, and heating apparatus put in place of the existing stoves, in 1912. The heating was lit when the temperature fell below 55 degrees Fahrenheit (12.7 degrees C). Electric light came to the church in 1950, and the electric organ was donated in 1988.

The Church in the Parish

Before the Norman Conquest, Rushbury Church may have served a larger area. It is somewhat oddly positioned at the south-west corner of the parish, which included the medieval communities of Rushbury, Wall, East Wall, part of Gretton, Wilderhope and the two Stanways, Stone Acton, and Lutwyche.

The combination of the four parishes has been a recent feature. The Rector of Rushbury took charge at Eaton in 1960. Then, in 1965, the parish was reorganised in the form of a 'plurality' with Eaton and Hope Bowdler. In 1968, Rushbury's rectory was sold and finally, in 1980, the order was made for the four livings, of Hope Bowdler with Eaton, Rushbury and Cardington to be 'held in plurality with one incumbent'.

Services and Attendance at Church

The Victoria County History records that in 1716 there were two Sunday services, one with a sermon, with Communion six times a year. Of the Reverend William Pemberton, Rector at the end of the eighteenth-century, it is said:

'He read prayers twice and preached once every Sunday, and always read prayers upon Saints' days. He administered the sacrament of the Lord's supper upon Good Friday and Easter Day, upon Whitsunday, at Michaelmas, and upon Christmas Day. There were about half a dozen communicants upon Good Friday and about thirty at Easter and near thirty sometimes at Whitsuntide'.

Wilderhope to Wall

His successor, the Reverend Starkie, tried to improve the services and their frequency and for a year he tried paying the singers. By 1849 there was Communion eight times a year; the congregation reached 150 in the summer but the poor roads and bad weather reduced it to 25 in the winter. Vestry records show that the number of communicants at Easter reached 83 in the last years of the century; Sunday services were then at 11.00am and at 6.30pm.

In the early years of the twentieth century, most children went to Sunday School (at the Methodist chapel at East Wall) and a high proportion of adults went to Church - some twice, possibly with a visit to Chapel in between. Sunday observance was strict.

The Rectory, the Parsonage House and the Glebe

The priest at Rushbury has been a rector since at least 1260. The name indicates that with the position, or living, there came some attached income, in Rushbury's case apparently both through tithes and through the glebe land. The glebe is the land set aside for the support of the parson, either directly through his own farming or by letting it to rent. The living of Rushbury was a good one, worth £14 in 1291 and £449 in 1851, both large sums at the time.

Rushbury was well endowed with glebe land; 50 acres in 1841 and 70 acres in 1856 and afterwards. In Rushbury, the glebe has always included the bulk of the south-western end of the low hill on which the church and parsonage house stand. Part has been known to modern generations as Parson's Bank; it was

The Rectory – circa 1930

Rector's Field earlier. There were once other areas of glebe on either side of Roman Bank above the railway and in what is now one very large field on the right of Eaton Brook downstream from the above.

There has long been a house for the parson on the Rushbury glebe. In 1589 it included farm buildings and a pigeon house. The house itself was described in 1793 as very handsome and an 1846 estate map shows three sets of buildings on the present rectory site, a long building alongside the road to the left of the present rectory gate, a T-shaped building above the sharp right-hand bend where the road from Roman Bank comes into Rushbury, and a smaller house where the Old Rectory now stands.

Hotham – Benson wedding gathering outside the Rectory on 5 May 1885

Wilderhope to Wall

The rectors have spent a good deal on maintaining the rectory. In 1820 it was recorded that 'Mr Starkie has laid out much money upon the Parsonage and grounds and made it very neat; but has destroyed the respectability by whitewashing good brickwork'. In 1852 the Reverend Hotham, who was shortly to restore the church, had the rectory remodelled and enlarged by the architect William Donthorn, something of a specialist in rectories although most his other work was in East Anglia.

By 1945 the Reverend Barrett had been finding the rectory difficult and expensive to maintain; indeed he proposed its division. The Vestry Minutes of 1951 are more optimistic: 'it gave us all great courage to see how the Rector had tackled the old house and put it into repair'; but by 1965 reality had intruded again. The present house could, it was hoped, be used for the rector of the new plurality, 'provided it could be modified and reduced in size at reasonable cost'. Rushbury's rectory was finally sold by the Church in 1968 and after a brief attempt in the late 1980s to turn it into a health farm it is now firmly returned to a private residence.

Working at the Rectory

The census records of the nineteenth century emphasise the wealth and social standing of the rectors of the time. In 1861 there were seven resident servants, including a governess and a groom. In 1871 the seven included a governess, a housekeeper, a nurse and four maids and even in 1881, when most of the rector's family had grown up, there were still five resident servants - a cook, three maids and a page. By the early twentieth century, the number of servants had been much reduced; older members of the parish today remember perhaps two servants - a maid and a gardener - in the 1920s.

The Church and Local Government

A look at the records of the meetings of the Church Vestry shows the very important part that the Church played in local affairs during the nineteenth century. The vestry meeting, under the chairmanship of the rector, set the poor rate and the Church rate, appointed poor law guardians, set the road rate for the townships of Rushbury and Wall, nominated parochial constables, appointed churchwardens, elected a way warden for the roads and on one occasion even set a rate for the cattle plague. All this came to an end with the Local Government Act of 1894 which transferred the main powers to parish councils.

RUSHBURY SCHOOL

Rushbury School was built in 1821 with money left in his will by Benjamin William Wainwright of Stanway. He directed that a school and a master's dwelling be built using £400 from his personal estate, a further sum to be invested and the dividends used to provide for a schoolmaster to instruct children in reading, writing and common arithmetic, and a schoolmistress to instruct the girls to knit and sew. What would he think of today's National Curriculum!

The state had no part to play in education in those early days and finance was taken care of by the income from Wainwright's Charity and voluntary contributions from the local gentry. Pupils also paid a weekly sum; labourers' children a penny or twopence and the children of tradesmen and farmers children, threepence or fourpence. Some poor children were educated free of charge.

Wilderhope to Wall

The nature of the school was altered considerably as a result of the 1870 Education Act. This act provided all children access to an elementary education, compulsory attendance following shortly after. Where there were no schools, school boards were set up to found and administer them. From now onwards there were determined efforts to ensure that Rushbury did not become a 'Board School', because of the additional rates that would be levied on the parishioners as a consequence.

The act also meant that Rushbury came under the umbrella of the Education Department. Applications for yearly grants had to be submitted to the department. The grant was dependent on the satisfactory report of H M Inspectors and, since this grant paid the master's salary, inspectors' visits played an important part in the life of the school. In July 1896 the inspector wrote:

'The children are orderly and their attainments are satisfactory in general, but there is a need of greater audibility and distinctness in the Reading and Answering. The Infants seem to be making progress, but the character of the Reading and Object Teaching should improve. Singing is hearty and Musical Drill is very fair but the songs might be rendered more sweetly. Some blinds are needed for the south windows'.

In the preceding years the school had been fortunate in having the Reverend F H Hotham, the Rector of Rushbury, (d.1887) as chairman of its trustees. He took a conscientious interest in the school, which extended to the payment of any annual deficit in the accounts. The Reverend Hotham also left a bequest to the school, so long as it never became rate supported.

Rushbury School grew considerably after 1870 and by 1871 there were apparently over 100 pupils attending. These children clearly could not be housed in the original small schoolroom and the Education Department insisted on improvements. The Reverend Hotham took the problem in hand, writing to the National Society to apply for a grant to build a new schoolroom with 'offices' and yards. The grant was refused, the lack of title deeds apparently posing a problem. An application to the Department of Education was decided against, perhaps because of the determination of the Trustees not to allow the school to become a board school.

The new schoolroom was built, nevertheless, in 1873 and future trustees were keen to point out that it was done 'without any grant of public money'. At this stage the school must have looked externally similar to the building of today. Inside it was very different. A wood and glass screen divided the room across the centre, separating the 'big ones' from the infants. One of the earliest memories we have is from Maggie Farr who started school in 1905, aged five. She wrote:

'I remember sitting at a long desk with steps to it, slates and slate pencils were used for writing on and rubbed out with a damp cloth or your sleeve ... the classroom was heated by a coal fire which had a guard round it and when the children got wet feet coming to school, socks were hung on the guard to dry when we put slippers on from out of a cupboard. Children had to walk to school, there wasn't a car or a taxi to bring them, some of them had to walk a long way. Sometimes after heavy rain there would be bad flooding on the road by the manor house and then the children were fetched by horse and cart'.

Class of 1905

When Maggie was eighteen she became a supplementary teacher at Rushbury school.

Wilderhope to Wall

Originally there were two almshouses built on to the side of the schoolhouse to house elderly widows of the parish. In the 1881 census it is recorded that the widows Martha Davies, aged 85, and Mary Beamish, aged 79, lived there. In the early part of the twentieth century these two tiny houses were made into one big room, used variously over the years as a parish meeting room, a library, a medical room and a dining room for the school.

The schoolhouse ceased to be used by the head teachers in 1971 and later became a rural base for a Wolverhampton school. In 1986, conversions were carried out by many volunteers so that the house came to be used as an extension of the school, with one upper room being used by the Rushbury and District Records Trust for their archives. Later still, one downstairs room was used by the Little Acorns, a flourishing playgroup.

An attempt was made to close the school in 1980 because of lack of numbers but a reprieve was granted in 1982 when children from Cardington School were transferred to Rushbury. The school today consists of an infant class in the original building and a junior class in a demountable classroom. Numbers now are 50 with an age range of four to eleven years.

Wilderhope to Wall

WALL UNDER HEYWOOD

A developing settlement within the Parish of Rushbury

At one time Wall was a small hamlet with three to four working farms, a blacksmith, two carpenters (one of them a wheelwright living between No 4 and Ivy Cottage), a butcher, baker and shoemaker. There were three shops, one of them - No 6 - a general and hardware store. Wall also had two pubs, 'The Plough' and

PC W J Trebble lodged with the two 'Miss Holders' in Wall.

the 'Lutwyche Arms', which was also the clockmaker's. Finally there was a post office and later a garage and agricultural engineers. Many people still remember Alec Evans, the barber, with his clippers and his promise not to 'hit him too hard'.

Wilderhope to Wall

One of the most significant changes must have been the construction of the by-pass taking the traffic, such as it was, from the village centre. Thirty years ago, one of the main sights in the village would have been that of a herd of cows going to or from milking. The 'foot and mouth' outbreak in the 1960s saw disinfectant-soaked straw across the ends of the roads to prevent spread of the disease. Except for Hall Farm, the other farms have disappeared. One farmyard has become a pleasant close of five dwellings, the remainder, at the time of writing, a yard of dilapidated buildings, but there is hope! Malt House Farm has a barn conversion and the old milking parlour, at one time a slaughterhouse, became briefly a pottery and part of it the post office. It is now a well-established school of dance and drama. The malting house was used as a village hall

The Plough Hotel as it was in 1942.

until the new hall opened in 1929. It then reverted to being a farm building and then a dwelling. What other changes have taken place? Well, the shops, carpenter, blacksmith and butcher have long since disappeared, together with the garage - now the site of three houses - and the 'Lutwyche Arms' in 1925. 'The Plough' has been much extended in recent years and is a well-known restaurant. There is still a post office in Wall, although its location has changed several times, as have the locations of the telephone box, now situated on Wall corner, and the post-box, now finally sited outside 'The Plough'. The house called 'The Old Post Office' was the original post office (also the shoemaker until 1930). It moved to the bungalow called 'Roman View' in Darby Lane, then to Malt House Farm, and finally to No 8 Wall, although this might change again soon.

Wilderhope to Wall

Chariot race at the 50th anniversary of the Village hall in 1980

Rushbury Village Hall is situated in Wall with 1997 seeing the construction and opening of the new hall to replace the wooden building of 1929. Prior to this, as noted above, the old malting house at Malthouse Farm had been the venue for social events. These and subsequent ones at the new village hall were often very formal with evening wear 'de rigeur'. Until 1920 an annual social event was 'Wall Wakes' held in a nearby field during the second week in June. This was a social and sporting get-together for the parish of Rushbury and visitors from neighbouring parishes. More recent events have been the 1977 Queen's Silver Jubilee, 'It's a Knockout' competition held in the field opposite 'The Plough'. I believe that Wall beat Cardington!

Maypole dancing at the Queen's Silver Jubilee celebrations

Wilderhope to Wall

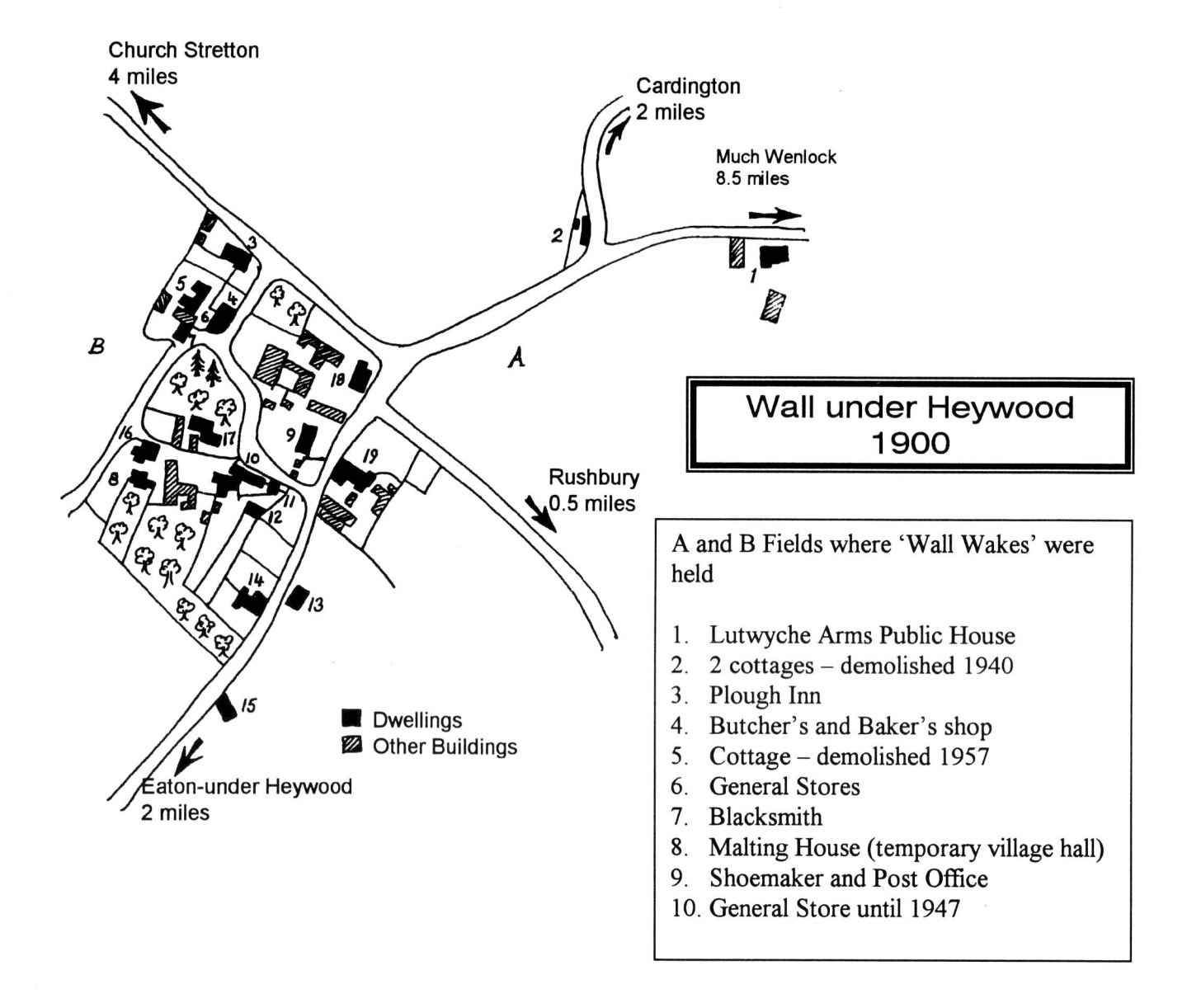

Wall under Heywood 1900

A and B Fields where 'Wall Wakes' were held

1. Lutwyche Arms Public House
2. 2 cottages – demolished 1940
3. Plough Inn
4. Butcher's and Baker's shop
5. Cottage – demolished 1957
6. General Stores
7. Blacksmith
8. Malting House (temporary village hall)
9. Shoemaker and Post Office
10. General Store until 1947

Wilderhope to Wall

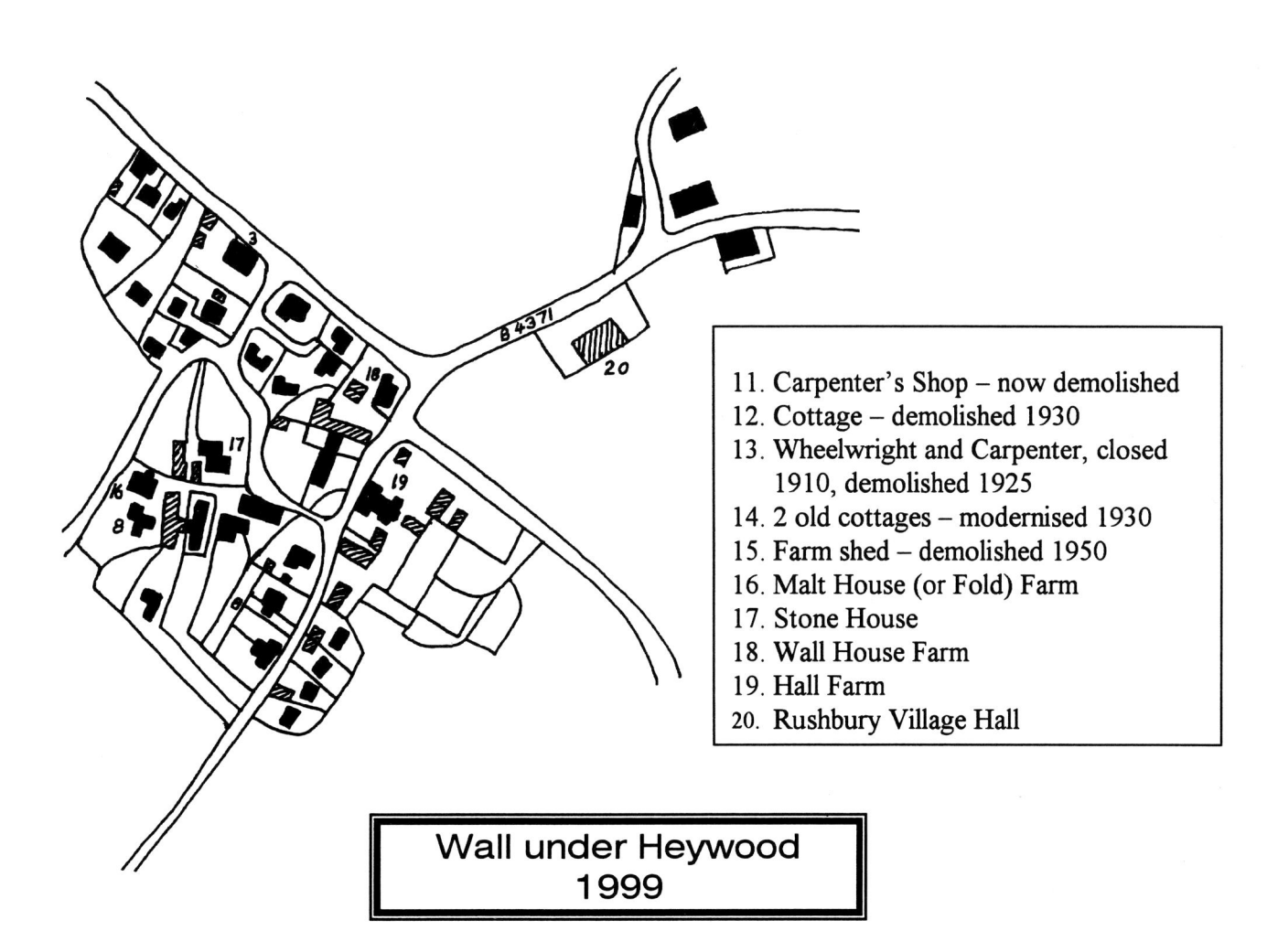

11. Carpenter's Shop – now demolished
12. Cottage – demolished 1930
13. Wheelwright and Carpenter, closed 1910, demolished 1925
14. 2 old cottages – modernised 1930
15. Farm shed – demolished 1950
16. Malt House (or Fold) Farm
17. Stone House
18. Wall House Farm
19. Hall Farm
20. Rushbury Village Hall

Wall under Heywood 1999

Wilderhope to Wall

Another occasion was the 50th VE anniversary concert in the village hall, celebrating half a century after the end of the second world war in Europe. The annual produce show attracts many high-standard entries. Rushbury and Wall have a history of sporting prowess – a football team, which played in Rushbury originally. It was an 'informal' team with no strip, no regulation boots, no goalposts, no set time for matches and no set number of players! It became more regulated in later years. John Webster recalls his time with the football team:

"It was I think in 1961 or '62 that John Boulton and I came to play football for the recently re-formed Wall United. Until then we had both been playing for the Coalbrookdale Old Boys, but the team had been banned from using the school field because of its over use; so, to Wall we came.

Our base was 'The Plough' (changing room in an outbuilding) and we played on Morgan's field behind the village hall. More organised than in the 1940s; goal posts (but no nets) now replaced the coats. The pitch was roughly marked out, but there were no corner flags. Our 'strip' was impressive, alternate stripes of dingy grey and white was worn with shorts of assorted colours. Boots were now purpose-made; heavy leather encompassing the ankles with studs nailed on. The ball also was leather, laced, and when wet, weighed a ton."

Expansion of the village began with the building of council houses in the 1950s. These were to house farmworkers and prevent rural depopulation. Since then houses have spread down Darby Lane and there has been infilling within the village itself. Rushope Nursery, which flourished in the 1960s and then closed soon after the owners left the area, is the site of the latest development.

Wall under Heywood is a village popular because of its easy access to the main Much Wenlock to Church Stretton road and no doubt will see further development in the future.

LONGVILLE IN THE DALE

Longville in the Dale is a small settlement in Ape Dale in the parish of Rushbury. It is within the Shropshire Hills Area of Outstanding Natural Beauty and consists of a loose-knit group of 25 dwellings with, at the time of writing, five family homes being built on the site of what used to be the auction yard. The yard was opened on 27 March 1913 for the sale of fat and store stock, the auctioneers being Nock Deighton and Kirby. They held fortnightly sales with local farmers walking stock into Longville. The sold animals would then be walked up the road to the station to go on the train either to Craven Arms or Wellington. The auction was closed in 1957 and the field then rented by two farmers, since when it has been sold to a developer.

Entrance to the railway station at Longville in the 1920s. The old Post Office is on the left.

Longville station was opened on 16 December 1867 and the last passengers stepped on to its platform on New Year's Eve 1951. Packages continued to arrive and depart for a further twelve years. The train was the main transport for farmers, bringing their milk by pony and float, like milk taken to Burgess at Birmingham or Wathes at Liverpool. The cattle feed came in by train for farmers to collect and the coal was stored for the surrounding area. In 1989 the waiting room ticket office was sold off with planning permission for conversion and extension to provide a three-bedroom home, but to date it still remains empty.

Mr and Mrs Archie Williams kept a post office for forty years. They started in a wooden bungalow in Slaughter House Road, then moved to the old weighbridge at the entrance to the station. Daily papers, sweets and cigarettes were the main sales, with a small quantity of groceries in the early years. When they returned, the post office moved to the Brooklands Garage, East Wall.

View of Longville village taken from the Plaish road. Home Farm is on the right.

The slaughter and knacker business was bought by Mr Michael Caine in 1924 from a Mr Bithell. At that time it was based in the old quarry this side of Wilderhope turning. In the late twenties they moved the other side of the bank where they remained until they ceased business at Longville. In the early years the animals were collected by horse and cart complete with a winch to haul the carcasses on. Meat in bins was taken to Longville station to go to London for the pet shops. Everything now goes to their only depot at Knighton, which is being helped run by the fourth generation of Caines.

Longville's main landmark is the 'Longville Arms', which for some years was known as the 'Station Hotel', then the 'Longville Hotel'. It was also a farm, the buildings now being holiday accommodation. Up until the 1970s they also had petrol pumps with a bell press on the outside wall which rang the bell in the bar. Saturday evening was the gathering night for fish and chips cooked in the redundant buildings. It is a pub that has seen a great number of landlords, the more recent concentrating on good food. In 1953 work started on the development of four council houses. In 1996 a redundant farm building at Home Farm was converted into living accommodation and a business selling bridal wear called 'Shropshire Country Brides'.

Longville has two farms, Longville Farm and Home Farm. Home Farm has been divided between three sons making Egremont and Longlea Farm with the Home Farm buildings being run as an agricultural contracting business.

EAST WALL

The hamlet of East Wall situated between Wall under Heywood and Longville in the Dale, had various owners over the years. In 1514 the Prior of Wenlock owned two farms, and the monks kept apiaries in this area (hence the name Ape Dale). They also had fish ponds in the dale and evidence of this still remains at Manor Farm. In 1578 other land was owned by Edward Lutwyche of Lutwyche, and Mrs Lutwyche was the principal landowner in East Wall in 1851. In 1858 Stone House Farm was owned by John James, a Manchester tobacco merchant.

Between 1870 and 1907 most of the properties in East Wall had been acquired by Abraham Haworth, a cotton broker from Manchester, and formed into the East Wall Estate of 1,045 acres, comprising seven farms, two smallholdings, eight cottages, blacksmith's house, shop and threshing contractor's premises and a retail butcher's premises with registered slaughterhouse and 57 acres of woodland. Mr Haworth employed an agent to administer the estate, and two workmen to keep buildings, gates etc in good repair. They had a workshop in the estate yard; it still stands today and is used as a store. When Abraham Haworth died the estate went to his four sons and carried on. They would visit their property, usually during the shooting season.

Threshing Machine and Austin tractor

On the death of one of the brothers in 1925, and to settle his estate, the East Wall Estate was put up for sale on 26 November 1925. In the sale brochure it was correctly described as a 'Finely Situated Agricultural and Sporting Estate'. Most of the occupiers bought their property at the sale and the unsold properties and the woodland were bought by a solicitor from Bridgnorth.

Soon after the sale of the estate the world-wide slump of the late twenties and early thirties hit this country and, as the saying goes, 'times were hard' during that period. All the farms in East Wall were mixed livestock and arable and were self-sufficient; in the main they were family farms with some employed workers.

Mr James Juckes was the butcher in East Wall. Circa 1900

At this time the depopulation of the countryside was taking place, and many people moved to find work in the towns and cities. This gave rise to the demand for fresh milk and as a result all the farms in East Wall turned to dairy farming as their main enterprise. They were well placed to do this. Longville railway station was only a mile away and on a level road. Each farmer took his churns by pony and float to catch the 8.15am train. The milk was transported for distribution mainly in the Midlands conurbation and Liverpool.

A thriving threshing and haulage contracting business operated at East Wall owned by Mr H Wooldridge; using steam traction engines they covered a wide area. Mr Wooldridge purchased the first self-propelled traction engine to come to Shropshire. Dick Bright drove it all the way from Lincolnshire. In 1910 the estate built two new houses for engine drivers, Nos 12 and 13 East Wall, and they were occupied by Mr H Medlicott and Mr R Bright respectively.

Mr Wooldridge also employed a full-time blacksmith, Mr Jack Edwards from Wall under Heywood, to shoe horses, repair farm implements and do general ironwork. Unfortunately, due to a tragedy, the business was run down and closed with a sale in 1939. The premises were then made into a garage and petrol filling station The blacksmiths shop, post office and village shop are now closed but the garage is still running.

The butchers' business run by the Juckes family retailed to all the adjoining villages. The slaughterhouse was closed in 1939 when war broke out, and all slaughtering was centralised. The business continued until the retirement of brothers Frank and Cecil, when the house and shop were sold and now form a private residence.

East Wall had a Methodist Chapel to which visiting preachers would come, usually by pony and trap. Services ceased in the mid-1930s and in 1939 the building was converted into accommodation for evacuees; the lean-to stable where the preacher housed his pony is now the kitchen.

Mains electricity arrived in 1950 as the National Grid was extended throughout the country. It was wonderful to be able to switch an electric light on and off as and when wanted. Hitherto paraffin lamps and candles were used and a few people had Calor gas. Oil engines were used to power barn machinery and milking machines on the farms.

The farms are now highly mechanised and large modern buildings have been erected. There are no work horses on any of the farms and less labour is employed. Much of the land is arable and some amalgamation has taken place, mainly growing corn; there are now only two dairy farms and one specialist pig farm.

In fact East Wall has remained largely unchanged. Only one bungalow and three houses have been built there since 1910. People now commute to work from East Wall to jobs outside the area.

STANWAY

The name implies a paved road which often has Roman implications and, given that the bridlepath from Hungerford has a stone base along much of its route and leads directly on to 'Roman Bank' thence down to Rushbury, itself mentioned in some local histories as the site of Bravinium, there may be some substance to this claim. Both Upper and Lower Stanway lie beyond Wenlock Edge in Hopedale and in the north-east tip in Corvedale and are not thus visible from rest of the parish. This, and a more sweeping easterly facing landscape, gives this part of the parish a quite different feel. The two Stanways were once joined by a network of roads which are shown on earlier maps, linking also with Wilderhope and Lutwyche. Communication now between these two settlements is via either of the two B roads in

Stanway Manor – from an old postcard dated 1910.

the dales. Whilst there is reference to a Lordship of Over and Nether Stanway in 1556 and a mention of the Manor of Stanway in 1621, no buildings of this period survive. The existing architecture is Victorian. The complex of farm buildings at Upper Stanway must have been the model of modern farming practice when built in the mid-nineteenth century. They were coincidentally built by an architect named Webb who was also responsible for designing signalling systems for the then new railways. These barns are now redundant owing to the changing nature of farming and as in many other parts of the country have been converted into dwelling houses.

Two of the inhabitants of the Manor in Upper Stanway were benefactors of the parish. Richard Wainwright formed a trust which, in 1841, built the school in Rushbury. Later, in the late 1920s, Mrs Williams, the wife of the then owner, a bookmaker, gave money to build the village hall in Wall. Her portrait, which hung in the village hall until recently, is now in the Rushbury and District Records Trust room in the school.

LUSHCOTT

Lushcott was once a small rural community with a chapel and possibly a school but little is known of those days. In 1891 all that remained of the community were two farms, Lushcott Farm of 144 acres and Little Lushcott Farm of 60 acres, both on the Lutwyche estate and farmed by tenant farmers. In the late 1930s a saw mill yard was formed along the track leading from Lushcott Farm to Wood Farm which was run by a Mr F Cartwright who lived at Paddock Cottages, Easthope. The yard was worked until 1941 when the agreement on the land ran out.

In 1937 Little Lushcott Farm was bought off the estate and on Monday 21 March 1938 Leonard H Davies, Auctioneer, held an auction at the Gaskell Arms Hotel, Much Wenlock to sell the outlying portions of Lutwyche Estate. In all it was about 1,277 acres and included in the sale was Lushcott Farm which sold for £2,000. The two farms at Lushcott were amalgamated in November 1953 and have remained so until the present day.

Lushcott Lane was fair game to the local young farmers in the 1960s. At this time a family with four daughters lived at Oakham Farm and when the girls returned home with their current boyfriends the young farmers criss-crossed the lane with baler twine. However what they forgot about was that the lane had two exits and the boyfriends didn't always return the same way. The farm labourers were not happy as they pedalled to work down the lane next morning!

Lushcott today is made up of five homesteads, Lushcott Farm, Lushcott Nursery, selling plants and shrubs to the wholesale and retail trade, two modern bungalows belonging to the farm and a cottage which was once Little Lushcott Farm.

Aerial view of Lushcott, showing the nursery greenhouses.

Photo: Clwyd/Powys Archaeological Trust

Wilderhope to Wall

WILDERHOPE

Nestling on the side of the Hope Dale on the borders of the parish of Rushbury is Wilderhope Manor, which was purchased in 1553 by Thomas Smallman, a lawyer. In the same year he also bought the neighbouring farm from Richard Parrimore, a London merchant. Wilderhope Manor is of the Elizabethan period and renowned for its fine plaster-moulded ceilings and oak spiral staircase. The house was occupied by six generations of the Smallman family, the most famous being Major Thomas Smallman who was a staunch royalist. He was captured by the Roundheads whilst taking dispatches from Bridgnorth to Shrewsbury and was imprisoned in his own house. But he managed to escape through a secret passage which led from the attic, down the garderobe (toilet) and out to the stables where he mounted his horse and galloped towards Much Wenlock. Unfortunately the Roundheads caught up with him and his only escape was to jump with his horse over the steepest point of Wenlock Edge, now known as Major's Leap. He managed to latch on to a tree but his poor horse was killed. Nevertheless, Major Smallman continued his journey to Shrewsbury on foot and delivered the dispatches safely. Thomas Smallman eventually sold Wilderhope Manor in 1734 to Thomas Lutwyche who owned the neighbouring estate about a mile away.

Wilderhope Manor

After Wilderhope's era

as the Smallman residence it became a farmhouse and the last tenants to occupy it were the Lippitt family who still live in Rushbury parish. In 1936 the manor house was bought by the W A Cadbury Trust from the Connell family of Much Wenlock and given to the National Trust. After extensive renovation by the Cadbury Trust the house was declared open as a Youth Hostel in May 1937. In the same year a new farmhouse was built. In 1971 the farm adjacent to the manor was also purchased by the Cadbury Trust from the Connell family and given to the National Trust. At this time Tony Dixon and his family were granted the tenancy of the farm and are farming sheep, beef suckler cows and cereals.

Fegg Farm which lies in the valley between Wilderhope and Lutwyche was part of the Wilderhope estate from 1785 to 1851. Until a few years ago was owned by the Connell family. It is now privately owned by the present occupiers, the Parkes family. They also farm sheep, beef suckler cows and cereals.

Although the Youth Hostels Association entertains more than 10,000 people each year at Wilderhope, it still maintains the manor's original charm and tranquillity and visitors often comment on the unspoilt beauty of the valley. A great majority of those visitors are schoolchildren who become most excited to find that they are staying in such a wonderful old house but usually it isn't long before the ghost stories start to pass around! Living next to the manor I have heard several tales of ghost sightings, but the most talked about is of a servant girl called Priscilla. Apparently she was very pale and thin with long black hair and would often sit on the servants' stairs crying. Those who allegedly spoke to her said that she was complaining of being very hungry and cold. As I have already commented, the manor is blessed with charm and tranquillity but in the darkness of night it can have a forbidding and sinister air.

Wilderhope to Wall

BUILDINGS AND ROADS

The pattern and mix of dwellings and farm buildings is typical of the rural areas along the Welsh border with local variations expected from this part of Shropshire. Although the Rushbury parish church is the only building surviving from the last millennium there are some interesting vernacular houses in local materials. A number of timber-framed buildings, usually combining local stone in their construction, can be found throughout Ape Dale. They are notoriously difficult to date, but the parish can be assumed to have examples from the fifteenth to the seventeenth centuries. These 'black and white' houses were, and largely remain, farms, often with a surrounding complex of barns in stone or, if they are of a later date, in brick. There are two in Rushbury village and equally fine examples in Wall, at the Coates and in Longville. One of the finest timber-framed buildings in the parish is Rushbury Manor with a tall, symmetrical front, great stone chimney stack at the south end and inside a half newel staircase. To the north of the parish are the two 'grand houses', Lutwyche Hall, built in 1587 by the Smallman family in brick and stone, and Wilderhope Manor, also built by the Smallmans but almost entirely in stone. Wilderhope is now owned by the National Trust and run as a Youth Hostel. Local quarries provided the stone for these handsome houses as well as the fair sprinkling of vernacular cottages and barns throughout the area which have no obvious dateable architectural features.

Rushbury Manor

The widespread introduction of brick houses appears to have been in the mid-eighteenth century with often only a token gesture towards prevailing national styles, but there are some identifiable Georgian buildings in the parish. The Victorians in the area have left a typical example of polychromatic brickwork in Stanway Manor and a 'Gothic Revival' addition to the rectory in Rushbury as well as two fine 'Italianate' railway stations, the one at Longville still in substantially original condition. There are again a number of other cottages and barns from the nineteenth century throughout the area. The school at Rushbury is interesting because although built in 1821 it is an amalgam of Classical and Gothic styles. The two surviving public houses, in Wall and Longville appear to be nineteenth century, presumably initially supplying the demand from thirsty farmworkers and in response to Victorian legislation

The Coates Farm – another fine example of a black and white timbered house.

promoting the consumption of ale as opposed to gin. Several of what are now private homes can lay claim to having been alehouses, notably the 'Romping Cat' on Roman Bank and the 'Lutwyche Arms' on the main road.

Wilderhope to Wall

The twentieth century has seen a scattering of bungalows, part of the first wave of urban re-population of the countryside, reversing the movement brought about by the mechanisation of farming and the reduction in demand for farmworkers. This has continued since the second world war with small housing developments in all the villages. This demand for 'executive property', fuelled by the seemingly insatiable desire by the urban well-to-do to live in the country, continues unabated. The subsequent conversion of all available ex-farmworkers' cottages has also been extended to barns conveniently made redundant by further changes in farming methods. There have also been in this last decade of the millennium farm relocations away from village centre sites with new types of farm buildings and modern farmhouses, often catering for tourists, with camp sites and bed and breakfast accommodation.

The parish is bisected by the B4371 Church Stretton to Much Wenlock road and briefly touched by the B4368 Corvedale road at the bottom of Slaughterhouse Bank, which connects these two 'B' roads. Roman Bank which also crosses Wenlock Edge to the south enters Rushbury over an attractive stone bridge guarded by two cottages, the one upstream purportedly was once a toll house. Maps tentatively support the building of this toll road during the late eighteenth century; it would have presumably replaced the sunken hollow way which crosses the Lake House Brook further downstream by a charming packhorse bridge. Whilst this bridge is widely referred to in local histories there are apparently no records linking these old parish tracks to wider mediaeval trade routes. The long distance Shropshire Way follows part of Wenlock Edge footpath which purportedly was a pilgrims route to the Cluniac priory at Much Wenlock. This is clearly shown as a substantial road on maps of 1808 and 1827 and is linked to a complex pattern of roads around Upper Stanway to Hungerford, Munslow and Eaton which remain in part today as footpaths and bridleways. They, like the wider parish pathways, are a legacy of earlier patterns of movement between villages, farms, church, schools and pubs. They are now enjoyed by local horse riders and large numbers of urban ramblers.

Wilderhope to Wall

THE TRAIN COMES AND GOES

It is hard to believe that, considering the great technical skill, huge amounts of equipment and hundreds of men required to build the railway, it was only an active part of the Wenlock Edge scene for less than a hundred years. The remaining cuttings, trackbed, bridges and converted buildings are but a shadow of what was once a thriving lifeline for the parish of Rushbury. A generation of people today still remember the days of the little steam trains with fond memories and closure of the line with regret.

The railway was built by a company called the Much Wenlock, Buildwas & Coalbrookdale Railway which was formed in 1860 and which three years

Rushbury Station and small pannier engine.

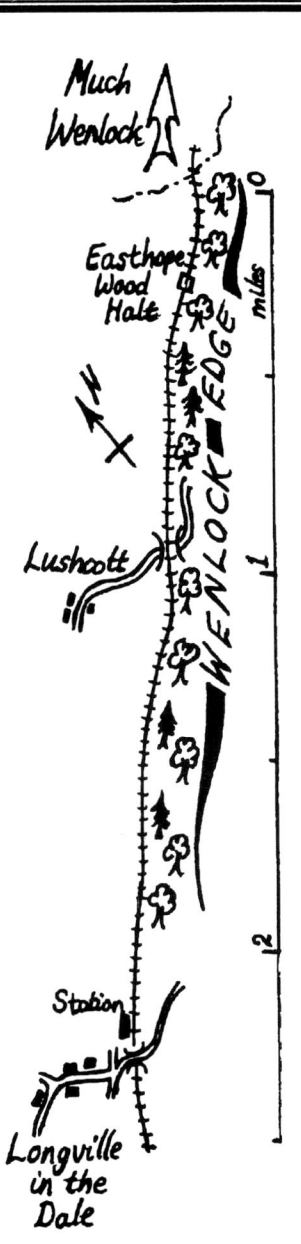

Wilderhope to Wall

later became part of the Great Western Railway. The Buildwas to Craven Arms line began in 1864 with a line extending from the West Midland Railway Branch at Buildwas to Presthope. The main purpose was to link the lime quarries there with the works of the Lilleshall and Coalbrookdale companies. In 1867 the line was continued under the Wenlock Edge, through a 207 yard-long tunnel connecting Hopedale to Ape Dale. The line now emerged into the gentler agricultural landscape under the escarpment. It ran through stations at the villages of Longville and Rushbury, eventually joining the Shrewsbury & Hereford Joint Line at Marsh Farm Junction, some 3¼ miles north of Craven Arms.

During its relatively short life, the railway made a large impact on the community. Its course ran the full length of the parish; road bridges and stations appeared at Longville and Rushbury; men found work as station master, porter or on the 'line gang'. Stations became little hives of activity as farmers moved their produce for sale and children made their way to and from school. The trains became the countryman's clock with the puffs of smoke down the valley indicating the time to knock off for lunch or finish for the day. A hostelry, known as the 'Railway Inn' and later as the 'Romping Cat', was built on Roman Bank, supposedly for the railway navvies; it is now a residence. In the early 1900s there were no telephones and messages for the vet were sent down the line to Craven Arms in the hope that someone would be passing his house.

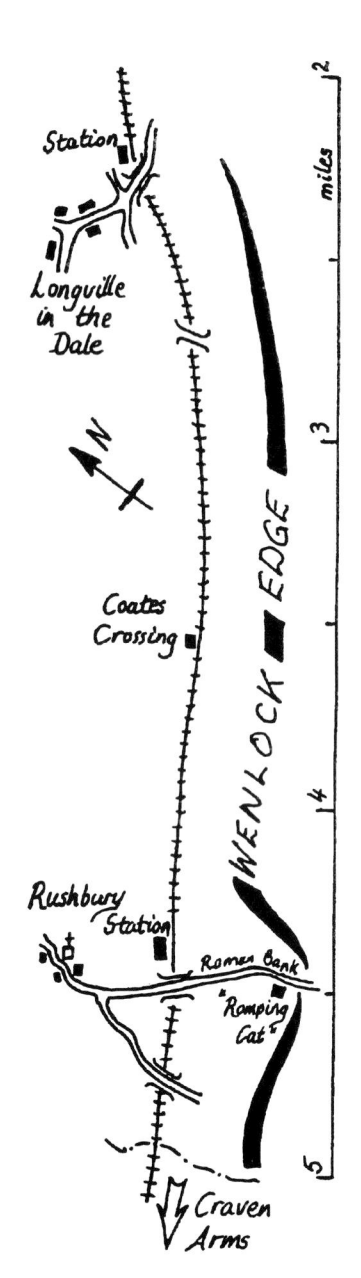

In addition to the stations in the two villages, there were other halts along the line, some more official than others! The Easthopewood Halt was the first stop in the parish, set in the steep-sloped woods and renowned for being very dark and eerie. In the winter, the guard on the 4pm school train would hang a tilley lamp on a platform bracket to brighten the gloom, collecting it on his return from Craven Arms. A stop would occasionally be made at the Lodge at the Coates Crossing - a perk for the stationmaster's wife after her shopping trips. Sometimes the train would travel slowly, especially through the woods. At this point the fireman might be seen, shovel in hand, chasing a pheasant or perhaps a rabbit or even picking mushrooms.

Milk churns at Longville Station in August 1932.   *Photo: National Railway Museum*

The movement of farm and local produce was an important feature of the railway. Both Longville and Rushbury stations had pens for holding cattle and sheep before loading on to the train. On Mondays there was a special farmers' train; a carriage for the farmers and cattle trucks behind to take their stock to

Wilderhope to Wall

Wellington auction. On a Monday also, farmers' wives would go to Much Wenlock market with their butter, eggs, rabbits and dressed poultry to sell them under the Guildhall. The local farms would deliver their milk daily to the stations in big churns that were destined for the industrial conurbations of Birmingham and Liverpool. Timber was another important local commodity and this was lugged from Stanway and Millichope to both stations.

Many local people recall travelling to school at Coalbrookdale on the train. In those days, the girls had to sit at one end of the carriage and the boys at the other. There was a train prefect on each carriage and no homework was allowed to be done on the train. At the end of the school day, those that lived beyond Much Wenlock would have to leave early and miss part of the last lesson to catch the train home.

Traffic on the railway increased dramatically during the Second World War with mainline locomotives hauling huge trains containing military equipment. This period, however, merely interrupted the slow decline of the railways as a whole. The railways were nationalised by the Labour Government in January 1948 and became British Railways. The short coal crisis of 1950-51 brought about the first cuts under BR control. Passenger receipts continued to fall and, by the end of 1951, the Craven Arms to Much Wenlock line was closed to passengers. The line was lifted between Marsh Farm Junction and Longville, which remained as a temporary freight terminus until 1963 when it was finally closed. When the lines were ripped up the sleepers were sold off for 10d each. They made good footbridges, fence and gate posts, and they are still in evidence in our fields today.

RUSHBURY VILLAGE HALL

Rushbury Village Hall was built in 1929 and run by a committee. The money was raised from local community efforts, with events being held at the Malt House, Wall, Manor Farm, Rushbury and other places in the locality. Mrs Williams of Stanway Manor was one of the main instigators and fundraisers. The Hall was built on land belonging to Wall House, Wall under Heywood. George Wyke gave the land but it was later legally transferred by Joe Madeley.

The committee was headed by two trustees but later, because it became impossible to find people prepared to take on the trusteeship, it was placed under the trust of the Parish Council and is now owned by the Charity Commission. The day-to-day running of the Hall is administered by a committee of locally elected management trustees.

The Hall is used regularly for Table Tennis, Badminton, Short-Mat Bowling, the WI and the Stretton School of Dancing. It is also hired by the YFC, the NFU, the school, and by individuals for private parties and weddings and many others.

The original hall was demolished in 1997 and replaced with a new hall and grounds with the assistance of a grant from South Shropshire District Council. As this book is being written, a new village green is being formed to celebrate the millennium on ground adjacent to the hall.

The old wooden Village Hall, replaced in 1997.

Wilderhope to Wall

RUSHBURY AND CARDINGTON WOMEN'S INSTITUTE

The Rushbury branch of the Women's Institute Movement was founded in December 1943 and monthly meetings were held in the Village Hall. As it was wartime, many activities centred around the provision of knitted items for the troops and, on the home front, an extra sugar allocation for jam making gave rise to the fun title of 'Jam and Jerusalem' for the movement.

Later, in 1972, the Cardington Branch amalgamated with Rushbury and thus became the Rushbury and Cardington WI. Nowadays, meetings are much more broadly based and include demonstrations, slide shows and talks on a wide variety of topics. Members also assist in a flourishing WI market which sells home-made produce, vegetables, plants and craft goods, and of course jam.

Membership has changed over the years and now embraces people from all walks of life, whereas in the early years it catered only for countryfolk. We have moved on.

The Rushbury and Cardington WI as Snow White and the Seven Dwarfs at the Church Stretton Carnival, 1997.

LONGVILLE BRANCH NATIONAL FARMERS' UNION

The Longville Branch of the NFU was formed in May 1939 at a public meeting held in the Longville Hotel. Thirty farmers and smallholders attended with Mr Watson Jones, the County Chairman, giving the address. The main aim of the movement was to further and protect the interests of its members and this remains today. During the war, the branch, together with the YFC raised money for the Red Cross by sales of livestock, donations and social events. In 1940, the subscription for members was 2d per acre, with a minimum of five shillings. It was said that this was easily repaid with the Union being able to arrange an extra ¼ d on a gallon of milk or 6d per hundredweight on beef or corn. In 1941, the branch agreed to an increase in subscriptions, because of the war, to 3d an acre with a minimum of ten shillings. It was also agreed that if a member could not be persuaded to pay the minimum, he would be allowed to pay a fee of 7s 6d, and gardener members not willing to pay more than the five shillings minimum would not be barred from the Longville Branch. At this time the average attendance at NFU meetings was 21. In 1945 it was decided to hold an annual dinner, a popular event which still carries on today.

Over the years a few changes have taken place: There are no longer guest speakers at the dinner and it is followed by the annual dance, traditionally held in the village hall. Originally, the secretarial work was a voluntary post but, in 1946, this became a full-time position carrying a salary and covering not only the Longville branch but also Bridgnorth and Much Wenlock branches. He is now called the Field Officer.

The concerns of the NFU in Longville have changed very little since 1959; that is, 'A fair price for a fair day's work', and 'looking after, to the best of our ability, the land which we farm to feed you'.

Wilderhope to Wall

RUSHBURY AND CARDINGTON YOUNG FARMERS CLUB

Rushbury and Cardington Young Farmers Club was formed in March 1939 at a meeting held in Rushbury School. A committee was set up with the support of local farmers who acted as an advisory committee and Mr Tom Perkins was elected as the first chairman. The annual subscription in those days was two shillings. Meetings were held at the Home Farm, Longville in a former egg room. Members of the time have fond memories of sitting on crates and sacks, with heating provided by a paraffin stove and the odd mouse for company.

1. David Williams
2. Alfred Jones
3. John Lewis
4. Bill Pendleton
5. Roy Williams
6. Bill Preece
7. Herbert Benbow
8. Cissie Phillips
9. Kitty Gibson
10. Stanley Gibson
11. Bill Rollo
12. Doreen Perkins
13. Beryl Gibson
14. David Taylor
15. Stella Gibson

1	3	5	7							14
2	4	6	8	9	10	11	12	13	15	

Meeting in the former egg room at Home Farm 1949

Wilderhope to Wall

Rushbury and Cardington YFC was one of the first clubs to join the Shropshire Federation which meant that they could participate in county and national events, thus adding to the interest. In 1949 they won the Annual Shropshire County Rally Challenge Cup.

1. Mary Griffiths
2. Doreen Perkins
3. Audrey Henderson
4. Cissie Philips
5. Stella Gibson
6. Beryl Gibson
7. John Lewis
8. Jim Madeley
9. John Speake
10. Margaret Benbow
11. Dulcie Henderson
12. Bill Preece
13. Frank Jones
14. Les Williams
15. Brian Lippitt
16. Betty Challenor
17. Lois Jones
18. Gill Gibson
19. Betty Preece
20. Charlie Davies
21. Frank Preece
22. David Taylor
23. Kitty Gibson
24. Stanley Gibson
25. Helen Mottershead
26. Rosemary Gibson
27. Herbert Benbow
28. Eileen Cox
29. Clifford Lippit
30. John Henderson
31. David Williams
32. Keith Mottershead
33. Jim Griffiths
34. Gerald Benbow

```
                    1   2
                  3   4   5
                     6
              7   8   9  10  11  12  13  14
           30 27 26 24 23 22    21    19    17 16
        34 33 31 28                20    18          15
              32    29    25
```

Wilderhope to Wall

In the early years calf-rearing was promoted and interesting talks were given on modern farm machinery, tractors for instance! Competitive events were popular and these included ploughing, beet hoeing, sheep-shearing and poultry dressing. Later, as the movement grew in popularity, debates, public speaking and drama were included as well as a great deal of fund-raising for charities.

The Club is now not only attracting members from the farming community as it did in 1939, but from all walks of life. With the help of its many ex-members now on its advisory committee, it is still helping the youth of the area to independence.

RUSHBURY AND CARDINGTON YFC – MEMORIES

Diana Taylor recalls her early memories of the YFC: My first memory of Rushbury and Cardington YFC is sitting in the morning room (front room) at home - Manor Farm, East Wall - listening to the not-so-tuneful singing of my favourite Christmas carols! In November 1968, the YFC put on an 'It's a Knockout' competition. I remember the event being held at Manor Farm in the field below the road, with the bottom part being used for a car park. Preparations started early with adverts in the paper for old unwanted pianos. These were stored at Manor Farm and were lovely, and the YFC was going to smash them to pieces! A marquee was needed, so my grandpa, Edward Turner (the seed merchant in Wellington), let them use the company show marquee. This was duly collected by Tim Brown, the then chairman, and my father, David Taylor. Chris Brown climbed the tent poles to attach the canvas.

As well as piano-smashing, there was egg-catching. A tarpaulin was slung between two elevators and eggs were supplied by the local hatchery. One person threw the eggs and the other had to catch them. There was also bedstead racing around a course laid out some distance from the other competitions. Tim and Simon Brown drove their double-decker bedstead at great speed around the course. I think David Mitchell from Brooklands garage also took part. I cannot remember who won that time but the Browns' bedstead went on to win many competitions.

Rushbury and Cardington also entered the Top Club Competition, a competition to put on a variety show. My first memory of this is a sketch concerning a bike. David Clarke was a car salesman and Philip Turner a bike owner. This bike was marvellous; it did and had everything. When I joined Rushbury and Cardington

YFC I was involved with Top Club. One year we won the county round, came second in the area round and went on to the semi-finals. This was the year of 'Jawsophine', a wire and paper shark on a hospital gurney. When we went to Tewkesbury with her, we were warned that the stage had a rake. Okay, we did not know what that was but Mick Pugh soon found out when he let go of 'Jawsophine' and she moved quickly towards the audience. When you have rehearsed every move to make things run smoothly, and suddenly you have to hold on to a rapidly moving paper shark with someone inside it, things just do not happen as they should. 'Jawsophine' went on to raise a lot of money when the club tied her between two tandems and pedalled her to the national AGM. She also took centre stage at the club's fiftieth birthday party.

In 1982, during the chairmanship of Brian Williams, the club decided to hold a marathon ploughing event. This was held at Mr G Jones' farm at Brockton. The ploughmen were Philip Lea, Robert Lea, Jonathon Benbow, Tim Madeley, Robert and Peter Jones, Brian Williams and Thomas Taylor. They ploughed for 24 hours, refuelling on the move and with the girls of the club running a caravan to provide food and drink. At the end of the day they just missed the record of the largest acreage ploughed in 24 hours, saying it was because they had to go into another field and travelling to the gate lost it.

An event that happens each year is the stock-judging rally. This is an event where members can practise their skills at judging animals, cooking and handicrafts. It is also a social get-together. Rushbury and Cardington YFC are one of the few clubs in the county to hold an event like this. The first one was held at Manor Farm, East Wall. The event in 1998 was held at Gretton Farm, the home of the joint chairman, Fred (James) Rogers. The only time the event was cancelled was in 1968 because of 'foot and mouth'.

This year the club has been working hard to fulfil the motto 'good farmers, good countrymen, good citizens', and through its members, having a good time and enjoying working together. They have managed to raise over £2,000 for charity.

In 1999 the club celebrates its sixtieth birthday, another event that will, no doubt, become part of its history, to be talked about with happy memories in the years to come.

Wilderhope to Wall

FOOD GLORIOUS FOOD

'Food Glorious Food', may be a well known song of today, but the meaning of such a statement would be quite different for a farmer's wife 100 years ago. Cooking was on the traditional black range, which also heated the water. Light was provided by oil lamps, with candles at bedtime. Central heating of course was unheard of in most households, so the feather bed, blankets, a bolster under the pillow and a chamber pot under the bed, were the norm. The only loo was the 'privy' down the garden, with newspaper instead of toilet paper to complete the task. Mixed farming was practised in the parish on over 40 farms and small-holdings at the turn of the century, with horses, cows, beet sheep and pigs. Chickens roamed on the cobbled yard and scratched in the mixen (midden) in front of the house.

Ale and cider was brewed on the farm (from apples bought in) usually with the help of a travelling cider press. Malt barley was also grown for the ale. Workers would fill their costrels (small barrels) and tie them to the horses hames while ploughing etc. Fields were small in acres but all had a name, Gladdies field after the Prime Minster Gladstone and Racecourse, which was once used for trotting races of the local farm ponies. Both these fields were at the Gilberries.

Life changed during the first world war. All able-bodied men over seventeen were called up, and most of the horses went too, so with both in short supply implements like the finger-mower and binder were acquired. Hay would be cut in June, turned by hand till made, then cocked in the field ready for loading on the dray to take to the stack-yard. Wheat and oats together with spring barley would be harvested from August onwards, with a horse-drawn binder. Sheaves were stooked in the field to dry for several days before being carried home to the farmyard stack, thatched, then left till later in the winter for threshing. The arrival of Wooldridge's Threshing machine from Lakeside (now East Wall garage) being driven by Dick Bright together with Harry Medlicott of East Wall Estates was quite an event in the year. Coal had to be fetched prior to the machine's arrival by the farmer from the station so, together with gallons of water, the steam engine could then be stoked to drive the belts on the box. Tom Evans was well known for slipping off the belts if he felt a rest was required. The threshing box and engine were set up alongside the stack, with one man on top cutting the strings and feeding the machine, while others threw him the sheaves. As the day progressed the vermin made their way to the bottom of the stack to hide, chicken wire was set up around the base (as the law required) and the 'mourners'* armed themselves with clubs and dogs ready for the kill. Threshed corn was carried in 2 cwt sacks to the granary. Surplus whole corn was generally bought by McCartneys who had a malthouse in Church Stretton (now the antique centre), after a sample had been taken prior to threshing, with money usually paid on account. Wheat was also taken to Gretton Mill to be ground into flour for bread-making. After all this physical work a huge amount of food and cider was consumed by all, hence by nightfall the mourners, who were usually half-drunk by now, were frisked for matches, before being allowed to sleep in the talent (loft) above the cows. A day's threshing with two men cost £2 5s 0d plus coal and food. Wooldridge's Contractors sold up in 1939.

> * Mourners - so called because they followed the box (threshing box) from farm to farm.

Cows were milked by hand up until the 1930s when a petrol-driven engine was used to run a vacuum pump. In winter they were tied-up by the neck in a shippon, with a boosy (glazed trough) for their food. Mangolds and swedes were pulped and mixed with corn and chaff, carried in a wisket (oval basket) and scattered down the line of troughs. Cows were also fed imported oil cake concentrate made by Bibbys and Silcocks, which was fetched from the station, mostly to keep them quiet while they were being milked. In 1933 the first lorry collection was introduced; the new ten-gallon churns were put on stands by the roadside for collection. This milk was taken to Bladen's Dairy at Dorrington, or Cadbury's near Leominster. These churns were sometimes used on out-of-the-way farms for keeping safe grocery deliveries, with dire

A cart full of swedes in the 1930s, accompanied by (left to right): Arthur Smith, Will Hotchkiss, Reg Edwards, Joe Madeley, Ron Bengree, and Harry Hotchkiss.

Wilderhope to Wall

consequences when not retrieved before milking. Cream was skimmed off every day and stored in a stein in a cool room, where once a week it was churned for twenty to thirty minutes by hand till it became butter.

The first telephone came to the area in the early 1930s, so improving communication with the outside world, especially if you required a doctor or vet. At about this time Will Johnson of Manor Farm, Rushbury was a leading breeder of shorthorn cattle, Kerry sheep and American bronze turkeys, the latter being exported to America in crates, especially made by Johnny Hollingsworth at the Gilberries. The outbreak of the second world war in 1939 brought another change to country life; people hosted child evacuees from the cities, swelling the school numbers. With all the men at war, land girls were employed by the larger farms instead. These girls were often from the cities, so were given four weeks training in the basics at agriculture college before starting work. German prisoners of war, stationed at Sheet Camp, Ludlow, were also deployed to work on the land. They arrived each morning in a lorry, which made a return trip in the evening to pick them up, while others lived-in with the families. Italian prisoners of war were in a camp at Presteigne, and these also worked locally. Some of these men married local girls and settled in the area after the war. Local Defence Volunteers, or as they later became known, the Home Guard, met at Rushbury Village Hall on Thursday evenings, with Major Seaton-Carr in charge. Each volunteer was issued

Local German prisoner of war

with a uniform, rifle, bayonet, hand-grenade and gas mask. With two or three men on duty each evening, they walked to look-outs at Stone Acton and Hazler Hill. Bombs were dropped during the war at Longville and Edge Wood, with at least six craters, but no casualties were reported except Mrs Cantwell's chicken shed at Stanway Lodge. Tom Perkins, Harry Lippitt, John Rogers and Jim Griffiths were in charge of the Lewis Gun. These guns were designed and built by Lewis Motley in a small factory at Barrow Street, Much Wenlock.

Wartime also brought rationing but, being a farming parish, most people got by with plenty of rabbits and home grown vegetables. During the winter most people, farmers and cottagers alike, killed a pig. A licence was required during this time to limit the number of pigs killed. It was usually two per household as food was rationed, but it was rumoured that the local policeman turned a blind eye to this with a bit of fresh pork to take home. Charlie Farrington from Diddlebury came on his butcher's bike, complete with his tools in the basket on the front, to ply his trade. After being killed the animal was hung on a gambrill in a convenient tree or building to set, before being butchered. Hams and flitches were carefully salted on slabs, while the bits were made into sausages, etc. Neighbours were given fresh pork, so when they 'killed the pig' the same amount of pork would be

Farm workers moved about the countryside on their bicycles. This is Norman Dale (our Parish Council Chairman in 1999) and his sisters returning from the fields in 1940.

returned. Ladies of the parish helped the war effort by collecting as much fruit as possible, before meeting at the village hall to make jam on their Primus stoves. Blackberries, whinberries etc. were picked by the children and sold to a dealer in Church Stretton, who, when he had a large enough quantity, regardless of the six inches of mould on the top, would send them to commercial jam-makers in the cities.

Moving on to the 1950s, the wonder of electricity came to the area, and life settled into a new routine. Although subsidies had been paid during the war, the 1947 Agricultural Act had been passed to enable a plentiful supply of food for the country, after the shortages of wartime. The aim of the act was that the producer had a fair price for his produce, while the consumer was guaranteed cheap food. Although mixed farming was still practised, livestock numbers increased. Tractors and combines replaced horse power, as labour was less plentiful, due to better wages being paid in town.

The 1960s and 1970s saw a steady increase in farm incomes; new buildings and milking parlours were installed on most dairy farms together with bulk tanks, to enable milk to be collected by large tankers. Britain joined the Common Market in the early 1970s and agriculture continued to prosper, resulting in over-production. In 1983 milk quotas were introduced to combat this excess. With a cut in milk production of twenty per cent, many small farms ceased to exist, with larger farms expanding and amalgamating. Beef and sheep production has also been restricted by quota. Cereal production did not escape the cuts; farmers had to set aside a percentage of their land to reduce the European grain mountain. Rushbury, like all other parishes, has had to conform to the system to survive the economic climate. During the last twenty years, we have seen intensive pig and chicken enterprises develop in the area, and even though this would be classed as 'factory farming' it enables several families to live and earn an income locally, which in turn keeps the school and parish thriving.

As we approach the millennium, agriculture has had to move forward to keep pace with modern life. Animals now have to have a passport since BSE so they can be traced from birth to slaughter. This involves many forms, so computers are now being used by all sections of the farming industry to keep records, etc. Unfortunately with all the restrictions and quotas, young people are unable to enter the industry except where the farm is handed down from a previous generation.

Land in the 1990s sells in this parish for between £2,000 to £3,000 per acre according to position and grading. Farmers wives today often go out to work to supplement the farm income, others diversify into small businesses run from home, examples of which are a bridal centre, plant nursery, caravan sites and bed and breakfasts, as the parish is situated in an area of outstanding natural beauty.

'Life is greener on the other side'; who says, most people think Rushbury is a wonderful parish to live in, both for its friendly people and its wonderful views. As some people who read this will not be familiar with agricultural practice, I hope this article will increase their knowledge and enlighten them. That life is not always easy no matter what industry you work in, and after, all the farm is our factory.

Sheep shearing in the 1990s at Manor Farm

Wilderhope to Wall

SHEEP WATCH by Joy Kohn

Fat slow-coach sheep that sweep the grass
With hour-hand stillness, still they pass,
And gently wear the field away,
Winding around their field all day.

Then dreaming eyes and drowsy ears
Refocus as a van draws near,
While shepherd fumbles for his key
Sheep turn to gather wearily.

Now greed is king; one ewe breaks rank,
Kick starts and hurtles down the bank.
Lamb like, huge bottoms leap and skip,
Flinging those stomachs down the dip.

In every sheep there lurks a lamb;
In every woolly dam and ram
Coiled beneath that fleecy skin
Lie muffled echoes of its spring.

Full filled with corn, abidingly
The flock re-cycles history,
Circles up hill, eyes down, lambless,
Embarrassed by such bounciness.

Jim Griffiths with the Gilberries Flock of Pedigree Suffolks

Wilderhope to Wall

MAP OF THE PARISH OF RUSHBURY

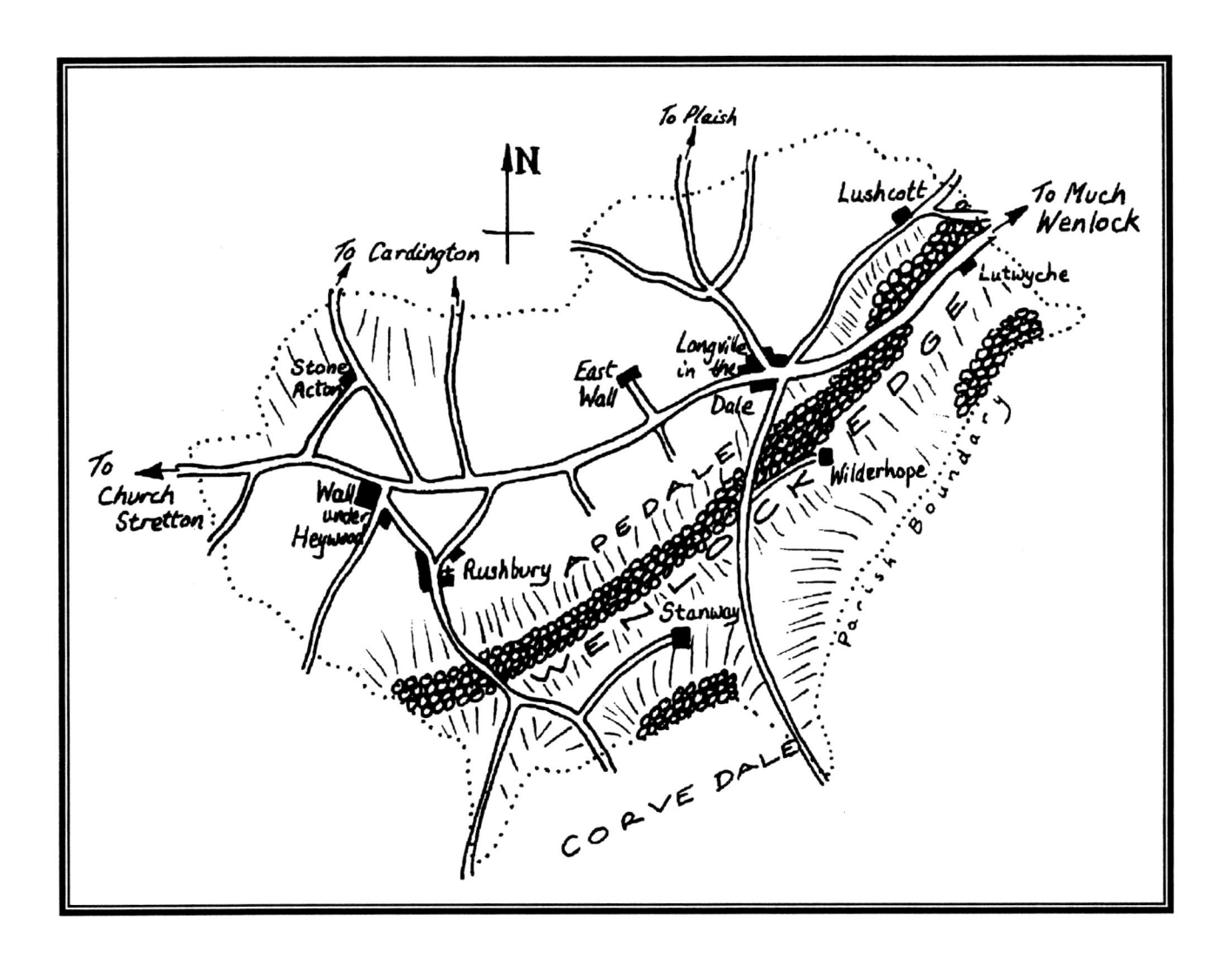

CONVERSIONS OF UNITS OF MEASUREMENT

The terms used in the text reflect the original usages, either from historical records or from the memories of the contributors. The following conversion tables will assist in reconciling these measurements with their metric equivalents of today.

Table of weight equivalents

1 oz (1 ounce)	28.35 g
1 lb (1 pound)	0.4536 kg
1 stone (14 pounds)	6.3503 kg
1 cwt (1 hundredweight = 112 pounds)	50.803 kg
1 ton (20 cwt)	1.016 tonnes

Table of distance equivalents

1 in (1 inch)	2.54 cm
1 ft (1 foot = 12 inches)	30.48 cm
1 yd (1 yard = 3 feet)	0.9144 m
1 mile (1,760 yards)	1.6093 km

Table of area equivalents

1 acre	0.4047 hectares

Table of £ s d (pounds, shillings and pence) and £ p equivalents

There were 20 shillings (s) in a pound (£) and 12 pence (d) in a shilling; so, £10 6s 6d would today be £10 32 ½ p. An old penny (1d) was rather less than ½ p today.